1ST CORINTHIANS FOR TEENS

1ST CORINTHIANS FOR TEENS

by

Bavly Kost

ST SHENOUDA'S MONASTERY
SYDNEY, AUSTRALIA
2015

1ˢᵀ Corinthians for Teens

ST SHENOUDA MONASTERY
8419 Putty Rd,
Putty, NSW, 2330

www.stshenoudamonastery.org.au

ISBN 13: 978-0-9941910-8-3

About the Author:

Bavly Kost is a Canadian Egyptian serving at St. George & St. Rieuss Coptic Orthodox Church, Toronto. Having completed his Education degree from York University, he then went on to complete his Master's in theology from St. Vladimir's Seminary. He currently works as a hospital Chaplain providing spiritual support for patients, family members and staff operating on a multi-faith basis.

Editors: Joseph Magdy, Andrew Gad

Cover Design:
Mariana Hanna
In and Out Creation Pty Ltd
inandoutcreations.com.au

Cover Design:
Hani Ghaly,
Begoury Graphics
begourygraphics@gmail.com

CONTENTS

INTRODUCTION

It has been over 20 years now since the death of Jesus. During these 20 years the Christian faith has been spreading throughout the Roman Empire. Major cities such as Alexandria, Rome and Corinth have established communities with many faithful leading the charge. St. Mark preached in Alexandria and Peter preached in Rome. However, many other communities are being established throughout Asia Minor (modern day Turkey and Greece) by St. Paul. Paul was born a Jew and was formerly persecuting the church (Acts 8.1). However, on his way to Damascus he had a vision of the Lord in which he changed his ways and began to preach about the crucified and risen Lord.

St. Paul now went around to different cities throughout the empire and began to preach to the Gentiles. He established communities in Galatia, Ephesus and Corinth. The community he established in Corinth was very dear to him (he wrote two letters to them). It was also a very important port city at the time so it served as a hotspot for many travellers and businessmen within the Roman Empire. Paul knew that this community is important for the faithful to remain strong and steadfast in the faith considering the amount of people coming in and out of the city. Paul knew that the community would go through a lot of difficulties. Paul begins the letter by mentioning Sosthenes whom he calls a brother. This would indicate to the reader that both Paul and Sosthenes wrote the letter to the Corinthians.

The letter to the Corinthians is addressing specific issues that either Paul has heard of or an individual has told Paul of. Paul then wrote in response to these issues to address the certain problems the church was facing. The issue of division and unity is addressed first (1 Cor 1.10-4.21). This issue forms the heart of the problem within the community. As other issues begin to be addressed they will focus around the theme of division and unity. Paul's main point in the first chapter is summed up when he says, "...be united in the same mind and same judgement" (1 Cor 1.10).

The community is clearly divided and Paul is trying to unite them together in same thought and judgement. People within the church were associating with various leaders and making factions that were dividing up the body of Christ. One way Paul points to this is when, he tells the community that were acting fleshly when they would take pride in their pastoral preference (1 Cor 3.4-5). Christ is the center and focus of the church and this is the starting point to all things happening in church. Unfortunately the community has lost sight of this starting point. St. Paul then addresses sexual immorality and its consequences upon both the individual and the community as a whole (1 Cor 5.1-13).

Paul is quite surprised at the lack of morality displayed by the Corinthians. This was probably due to their contact with people who travelled in and out of the city. The fact that the community was able to tolerate a man who was committing sexual immortality displays the amount of surprise St. Paul had when writing the letter. The Apostle makes it clear that this type of action is not to be tolerated but disciplined in order to bring the individual back into the body of Christ.

CHAPTER ONE

Events

CHAPTER ONE

INTRODUCTION

Okay, so let's read chapter 1. What you may have noticed, is that St. Paul starts most of his letters in the same way. He starts with a general greeting and then delves into the main issue. In 1 Corinthians, the main issue is that of division, and we see this in verse 12. Some people had become fans of St Paul, others had become fans of Apollos, others were saying they were supporting Cephas– they had all forgotten that Christ is not divided. Instead of worshipping God in unity, they ended up forming smaller competing factions, thereby dividing the Body of Christ (which is the church). St. Paul thus tells the community to have one mind and one purpose.

A HOUSE DIVIDED

Christ Himself warned that a house divided against itself cannot stand. He even said that if demons are divided against themselves then they wouldn't stand. And it is so true! Have you ever been in a sports team where the players don't get along? Or there are too many individual stars that aren't willing to compromise themselves for the sake of the team? More often than not, the teams of individual stars will and up beaten by a team of less talented co-operative people.

So why does this division start in the first

place? Often the root is pride. Pride stops us from putting others in front of ourselves. It stops us from being united, because my ego overrides others.

So how do we solve this issue..? One thing we can practice for today is to put others first. Let's remember the example of countless holy people who put others before them. Mother Teresa chose to offer herself completely to serve in a foreign country. She put away any pride or any ego, and sought to completely serve God's children. Of course, the true and perfect example is our Lord Christ! Our eternal God chose to take human flesh, be born in the depths of a manger, be despised by many, and end up crucified among thieves– all for you and me.

GOD'S MIGHTY WORK

St. Paul writes that God has chosen the 'foolish', 'weak' and 'base' things of the world

What the Fathers Say

"By saying "called to be an apostle", he means to say: What I learned was not my own, but I was called while persecuting the church. And God intends for you to be saved by the same way; for we have done nothing good on our own, but were saved by the will of God"

– St. John Chrysostom

People, Places &Things

'Called to be Saints'

One of the most common names for all the believers in the New Testament was 'saints'. When we think of saints, we often think of St. Mary, St. George and many others. But a saint is not just someone mentioned in the Synaxarium. We too are called to be saints!

The word 'saint' means 'holy one', a person who has been set apart for God. In the Holy Liturgy, the priest says: 'the Holies are for the holy people'. Therefore, we are chosen by God to become holy people, to become saints and to live a life different from the rest of the people on earth.

to put to shame the 'wise' and the 'mighty'. These might seem far-fetched, however, there are several examples where God's might gave many people unlikely victories.

In the book of Judges, the story of Gideon and the war against the Medianites is the perfet example. The Medianites were 135,000, while Gideon and his men numbered only 32, 000. If this wasn't bad enough, God told Gideon to ask those who were unwilling to go to war to return to their homes. 20,000 returned home, leaving only 12, 000 to fight war. Even after this, the number decreased again. God asked Gideon to take the Israelites to the river, where those who got on their knees and drank of the water were to be sent home. Only those who lapped the water, putting their hands to their mouths, were heading to war. Only 300 remained. If it was unlikely before, it now seemed almost impossible that 300 men could defeat 135, 000 Medianites! However, God chose the little, the insignificant and the weak and made them strong, giving victory to Gideon and his 300 men.

REFLECTION

How often do I think of my own short-comings and weaknesses instead of remembering God's love and mercy? Let's focus on God's strength, and not our inability

ST PAUL'S PROFILE

Born: 2 BC

Died: 67 AD

Birth Name: Saul

Heritage: Jewish, of the tribe of Benjamin. He was a Pharisee.

Occupation: St. Paul was a tentmaker for a living.

Birthplace: Tarsus (modern day Turkey)

Early Life:

He was a very zealous Jew, and studied the book of Torah in much depth. He persecuted the Christian church, and guarded the clothes of those who were stoning St. Stephen.

Conversion:

As he journeyed near Damascus, a great light fell from heaven which blinded Saul and he heard a voice: 'Saul, Saul, why are you persecuting me' Saul replied: 'Who are You, Lord?'. The Lord said: 'I am Jesus whom you are persecuting. It is hard for you to kick against the goads' (goads are spikes used to poke farm animals. God basically meant that Saul is fighting against the divine truth). Saul was then ordered to go to Ananias in Damascus, who baptised him and he received sight.

His Work:

St. Paul is considered amongst the most influential figures in the development of Christianity. He wrote 14 epistles, more than half of the New Testament. He is often referred to as 'the apostle of the Gentiles' and established churches in Corinth, Ephesus, Asia Minor, Rome and many other cities around the world. He went on three missionary journeys preaching the world to all nations.

Death:

Emperor Nero seized St. Paul in Rome, tortured him severely and eventually ordered that his head be cut off. This concluded a life of struggle and torture for the sake of Christ.

CHAPTER TWO

CHAPTER TWO

THE MIND OF CHRIST

St. Paul begins this next chapter by clearly stating his intention of only wanting to know Christ and Him crucified when he came to the community. The way St. Paul came speaking to this community is through the wisdom of God. He makes it clear that this was the wisdom of God and not of men. He stresses this because the community is probably being given information that is not from God. St. Paul goes on to say that the wisdom he speaks with was given to him and to us all by the Spirit. In the final verse of the chapter, Paul reminds us that "we have the mind of Christ". That is something that should always come out in all our actions. But what does it mean? And how can this happen?

KNOWING CHRIST

Think about your closest friends. Have you ever looked at each other in a certain situation and felt that you knew exactly what they were thinking. Almost as though you could read their minds? Any time you spend a lot of time with a close friend, you almost develop a telepathic friendship. Likewise, when we spend more and more time with Christ, we can become imitators of Him more.

This relationship is evident in many of the saints. How did Pope Kyrollos seem to know things from the future? How did he seem to know secrets of people even before people would say them to him? Sometimes he would confidently tell a barren couple if they would have a kid soon. He would even tell them if it was a boy or a girl! How did he dare to do that? Because he had spent so much time in God's presence. He had the mind of Christ, and was always focused on Christ. Just like we are in tune with our best friends, Pope Kyrollos was in tune with God. We too have been baptised, are part of the church and have been given the mind of Christ. We have been given the same invitation. So let's try to keep our mind focused on Him, and tuned on Him.

THE SPIRIT OF GOD

St. Paul says that we have received the 'spirit of God' and not the 'spirit of man'. An important distinction needs to be made

What the Fathers Say

"If the Holy Books drew men to faith because they are written with eloquence and philosophical cleverness, our faith would undoubtedly be based on words and human wisdom, more than it is on the power of God"

– Origen

People, Places & Things

'Eye has not Seen, nor Ear Heard'

In verse 9, St. Paul describes the spiritual wisdom and the word of God which 'eye has not seen, nor ear head. Nor have entered into the heart of man'. This points to the prophecy mentioned in Isaiah 64:3, and is a phrase mentioned every single liturgy in the gospel when we 'pray that we may become worthy to hear and to act according to the holy gospel'. When Moses wanted to see God, God only allowed Moses to see His back since 'No one can see God and live' (Exodus 33: 20). We should feel privileged and honoured to have the word of God, the Bible, as our spiritual food and never take this for granted.

between the two. For the spirit of God is one which reveals signs and wonders, leading spititual people to repentance and bringing them closer to the kingdom of heaven. Whilst following Christ's footsteps may seem difficult at first, the Holy Spirit is what strengthens us: 'Come all you who are burdened and heavy laden and I will give you rest'. Meanwhile, the spirit of the world is one full of pride, bodily lusts and wordly pleasures. This is a wide path which many people fall in, and leads to suffering both here on earth, and in eternity if we do not repent of our iniquities.

The spirit of God was upon David the prophet, and God even described him as 'one after my own heart'. Even though David commited adultery with Bathsheba and indirectly murdered her husband, he came to his senses and repented a true repentance. He said 'I drench my bed with my tears' and 'all night I make my bed swim'. Let us pray that the Lord God provides us with the ability to arm ourselves with the strong spirit of God and overcome the pleasures of the world.

REFLECTION

Make a conscious effort to remember God throughout the day. All it takes is a quick arrow prayer: "O my Lord Jesus Christ have mercy upon me a sinner"

THE LETTER TO THE CORINTHINAS

Date Written:

> 54-55 C.E, during Paul's third missionary journey, toward the end of his three years ministering in Ephesus.

Author:

> Both 1 and 2 Corinthians were written by the Apostle Paul. He established the church in Corinth, and was proclaimed the fathers of the Corinthian believers (1 Cor4.15). Also in both letters Paul signs the letters written by the Apostle (1 Cor 1.1 and 2 Cor 1.1).

Setting:

> Asia Minor region (Modern day Turkey and Greece). The young Church in Corinth was located in the midst of a large seaport-a city deeply immersed in pagan customs. The believers were primarily Gentiles converted by Paul on his second missionary journey. In Pal's absence the church had fallen into serious problems of disunity, sexual immorality, confusion over church discipline and other matters involving worship and holy living.

Major Themes:

- The Church

- Unity among believers

- Spiritual Freedom

- Ressurection

- Sexual immorality

- The Eucharist

- Marriage

CHAPTER THREE

CHRIST AS THE FOUNDATION

St. Paul begins the chapter by telling everyone in the community he has to speak to them as if he is talking to infants. He says this is the case because had he spoken to them as adults they would not have been ready. Paul then proceeds to bring back a reference he made in chapter one. He brings himself up and Apollos. He is speaking to those who said "I am of Paul" and "I am of Apollos". He goes on to say that they did come to them and speak however it was the work of the spirit who brought them to the community to preach in the first place.

Paul says that he laid the foundation for them but it was truly Christ who was working to aid them in their journey. It is Christ who is the ultimate truth. By placing our hope in Christ we come to see the true light which enlightened the world on the cross. Trusting in anything that stands outside the body of Christ distorts the image of truth. It is in truth that we find life and life is found in Christ as he said, "I am the way the truth and life" (John 14.6). The issue of pride was central in this community because Paul concludes this chapter with this notion of pride. This clearly bothered Paul and he had to bring it up again. The central point that we can take away from this chapter is the theme of building.

CHAPTER THREE

WHAT DOES IT MEAN TO BUILD?

The word "build" shows up a fair few times in this chapter, in verses 9-17. St Paul uses this analogy, that we are God's building, and that everyone who serves is invited to help build. This is the concept of "synergy". God, in His humility, allows us to become fellow workers with Him. We build many things throughout the course of our lives. We build up our education, our bodies, our homes, relationships... and in any of these, the foundation is vital. If there is a slight problem at the foundation, it can spell disaster for everything on top. The same thing applies in our spiritual lives, and St Paul seeks to emphasise the importance of the manner in which we build up our foundation. We must

The Missionary Struggle

The Corinthian people were divided and some claimed to follow Paul, others Apollos and others Cephas. However, the three men were all united in their teachings and it was rather the Corinthians who were stubborn and refused to acknowledge this.

Wouldn't it have been so much easier if St. Paul could just take off on a plane or even drive to Corinth, settle the disputes and then continue preaching elsewhere?

However, the main source of travel was walking. Some scholars have estimated that St. Paul travelled over 20, 000 km by foot over the course of his life.

People, Places &Things

lay out the plan and know what the course of action is.

St. Paul urges the community of Corinth to lay their foundation through the Spirit. What does that mean? It means that we must be confident in our ability that God has bestowed to us. We all have many talents and we must learn to utilize them in order to get the best out of us. This can only begin by laying the foundation and then growth of this foundation will continue through the work of the spirit.

This is similar to the famous Parable of the Talents. This parable, which Christ told us, is an example of how to lay down a foundation and let it grow. We see the first two servants taking the talents that were given to them and they let it grow while the third servant buried his talent out of fear that he might not gain much with it. We must be like the first two servants. As much as we are given we must learn to work with it in order that others might see Christ in us. By laying this foundation it will allow us to grow in the person of Christ and be filled with the spirit of love.

FOOLS FOR CHRIST

In vs 18, St Paul gives us all a warning that we should heed. He says, "Let no one deceive himself... let him become a fool that he may become wise" This is a vital lesson we should all learn. It is vital that we be humbled and not get upset about it.

There is a famous story that is said of St Macarius. One day he told one of his disciples to go to a nearby cemetery and praise the dead people there. So the disciple went and praised them, then returned to St Macarius. St Macarius then told him to go back and insult all the people in the graves. So the disciple obediently went and insulted the people in the graves, then returned to his teacher.

St Macarius then asked his disciple, "What did the dead people do when you praised them?"

The disciple responded, "They did not react."

"And what about when you insulted them" asked St Macarius.

"They didn't react either" responded the disciple.

St Macarius then said, "See? That is how we should be. Whenever someone praises us or insults us, we should not react". We should not allow people's praise to make us get big heads, and neither should we allow insults or criticisms to hurt us.

There are many other saints who discovered this. They chose to "become a fool that they may become wise" just as Saint Paul said. They were happy to let people think that they were crazy, so that the praise of men would not affect their spiritual lives. St Anna-Simone is one such saint. She was a

What the Fathers Say

Look at how he rejects to be worshipped, as though he is in the position of Christ! Although planting and watering are both great achievements, yet, he confirms that he who plants, or he who waters, are nothing; refusing to refer to himself any role in the salvation of those he intends to edify in Christ.

- St. Augustine

What the Fathers Say

I am not in favor of comfort, but I prefer the perspiration of labor, which is more glorious, according to the apostle. He who does not do what his energy qualifies him to, will certainly be punished.

-St. Gregory of Nyssa

princess, who left all to become a nun. When she joined the nunnery, she acted like a fool, and all the other nuns thought she was crazy for years. She knew, it was safer for people to think she was crazy, than for people to start praising her, lest she become proud or puffed up. It was only some years later, when the Lord chose to reveal her blessedness, that people realised that she was actually a saint.

If these great saints all recognised the dangers of pride, then how much more should we realise it!

REFLECTION

How often am I influenced by other people's opinons? Lets learn to ignore both the praise and criticism of man and focus on pleasing God.

CHAPTER FOUR

CHAPTER FOUR

JUDGEMENT AND PERSECUTION

St. Paul begins this chapter on a strong note. He speaks about judgement and judgement of himself. It seems like many within the community were quick to judge Paul for his actions and teachings to the Corinthians. St. Paul goes on to announce that they all have become kings. Not kings in the worldly sense but in the knowledge they have received from Apollos and himself. Then he goes on to say he wishes he too can be a king. This is more of Paul taking a jab at the community saying that he wishes he had received this knowledge a lot earlier but he did not.

St. Paul then goes on to say that himself and Apollos have given everything they have for the community. They have been beaten up, persecuted and dragged on the streets for the faith they have preached to them. He wants them to be aware of what they have because many people have died for this faith which they have taken very lightly. St. Paul says all of this in order that the community can be imitators of his actions. St. Paul is stressing the fact that we have to be hard workers in order to strive for God's kingdom.

In saying all of this, St. Paul is encouraging those within the community to also work hard and persevere so that they might bring their work together in the body of Christ. St. Paul is trying to tell the community and we can understand it the same way is that persecution and suffering are steps taken to the kingdom. The kingdom of Christ is one that is constantly being worked for. St. Paul says that we are constantly working out our salvation and this is the message he is trying to get across to the Corinthians and this is how we are to understand it as well.

WHAT IT MEANS TO BE A DISCIPLE

An important take away message from this chapter is discipleship. We all must have role models that we look up to. We have previously mentioned the importance of a spiritual father. Besides having a spiritual father I think it be healthy to also have someone you look up to and get advice from when we can. In this chapter St. Paul gives us

Role Models

St. Paul writes: 'I urge you, imitate me'. However, he takes no pride in himself and even calls himself the least of the apostles, not worthy to be called an apostle. Instead, he means that as Christ is the centre of his life and the focus of his ministry, so too should we have the same goal. It is good to have role models on earth, but most importantly, Christ should be the major focus of our life.

People, Places &Things

the example of Timothy who was St. Paul's disciple. On a personal level I have a good friend who is a few years older than me and I stick to him like glue. We hang out a lot and we constantly challenge each other to be critical thinkers.

It is important to have a good core group of friends because if your friends do not challenge you on your views then pride would begin to build up. You will start to think everything you contemplate on is correct and this is simply not true. We need people to watch over us and to take care of us. There are countless examples of people within the church who have had role models whom they consider having a huge impact on their lives.

A modern example would be Pope Shenouda and Pope Kirolos. They both had Father Abdelmessiah el-Habashi as their mentor when they both entered the monastic life. Our friends and friendships have the power to form us and it is important

What the Fathers Say

"Paul was worthy to become a spectacle to angels, having strived to gain the reward of Christ; he struggled to set the angelic life on earth, by wrestling against the spiritual wickedness"

-St. Ambrose

'We are, you are'

'We are fools for Christ's sake, but you are wise in Christ. We are weak, but you are strong. You are distinguished, but we are dishonoured'. Irony and sarcasm are bitter medicine, and St. Paul uses them both to criticise the Corinthians.

He compares the apostle's life of poverty and struggle with the relative comfort of the Corinthian community. How often do we likewise happily remain in our comfort zone and never think of serving others.

to ground ourselves with a good core group of friends who watch over us and can lead us back if we ever grow prideful.

What the Fathers Say

"Paul knows that although his heart was still prone to sinning, yet his actions were upright"

–Origen

REFLECTION

Am I a disciple to my confession father? Or do I at least take his advice on board? Let's organise our spiritual life and make sure we see our confession father at least once a month.

ST PAUL'S MISSIONARY JOURNEYS

After St. Paul's conversion, he went on three missionary journeys preaching the word of God to the Gentiles. As you can see from the map, St. Paul made several journeys throughout his life. However, he didn't have the luxury of planes or even cars to travel with. He had to travel from city to city on foot or on horseback to preach the word of God to all nations.

This map shows the three missionary journies of St. Paul. His first journy beginning at Antioch and running through Asia Minor going to Galatia, Corinth and other major cities of the Roman Empire.

St. Paul's second missionary journey began at Ephesus and ended at the city of Corinth and this is when he wrote his first ever epistle, the letter to the Thessalonians. It was on this second missionary journey where St. Paul established the Christian community in Corinth.

This map also shows his third and final missionary journeys of Paul. He spent two years in Ephesus where he heard of the problems at Corinth, and wrote his first epistle to the Corinthians. His final missionary activity ended in Rome, where he was killed by the Roman authorities.

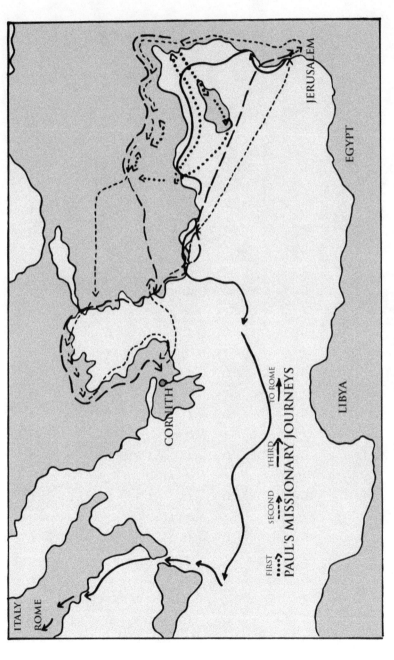

Map of St Paul's Three Missionary Journeys

CHAPTER FIVE

CHAPTER FIVE

THE LEAVEN AND THE LUMP

Chapter five focuses on the topic of sexual immorality. The city of Corinth was a port city and being a port city it saw many people come in and out. Paul is writing concerned that those who are caught up in this sexual immoral behaviour are affecting the community at large. Paul uses the analogy of the little leaven (or yeast) destroys the whole lump and warns against this kind of behaviour. Today we are living in a fast paced society were we are constantly being bombarded with pictures, and media outlets that it makes it a hard task to filter everything we see and hear. Paul's solution is simple and to the point-to cut ones selves away from these people. This is the same solution for our modern times. Not that we should cut away from people completely but rather learn to love the person who stands in front of us.

Who can ever say no to Christ's message of the good news? If we learn to live out the word of Christ those around us who cannot see Christ will learn to see the good in us and will ultimately use that to their benefit. We must be strict and quick to cut out the things that prevent us and take us away from Christ but we must be able to discern how to use the culture and society around us to bring the good news to all.

Many stories of the monks dealing with this kind of behaviour have been told to us in Sunday school. One particular story that resembles this is with St. Moses the Strong. He was asked to join a council to judge a younger monk of his sins. So he got up and began to walk with a bag full of sand which had a hole in it. He reached the council and dropped the bag. They asked him what this was and he answered them that these are his sins that he carried and that if they were to judge anyone they should judge him first. All the monks asked St. Moses for forgiveness and did nothing to the younger monk. If we are aware of our sins and learn to use that as our motivation to be united to the body of Christ then every interaction we have with other human beings will be an interaction of peace and love.

It is only in the body of Christ that we can live out the message of Christ. Christ is presented to us through the Eucharist

What the Fathers Say

In contradiction, the perpetually hated impurity puts an ugly and filthy stain on him who has it, sparing neither his body nor his soul of its defilement. Because once it prevails, it makes man utterly under the yoke of its covetousness ...

It usually starts with seduction, and ends with a great destruction of the soul that it seduced.

- St. Cyprian of Carthage

Sexual Immorality

One particular incident which shocked St. Paul. There had been reports of man lying with his father's wife! Such an event was completely unheard of to St. Paul, even amongst the Gentile community. The Corinthians did not know how to deal with the situation. However, St. Paul advised to take a clear stance against this sinful man, because he continued to cause unsettlement and repentance had escaped from his heart.

People, Places &Things

which was made possible in the truth of Christ through his resurrection. Christ conquering of death allowed us to participate in the body of Christ as the community of believers.

SEXUAL IMMORTALITY

We see a shift now within the epistle as chapter five begins to deal with specific issues that the community in Corinth was dealing with. Sexual immortality was an issue that St. Paul sought to correct. He does so by showing to the community that life is an enjoyment of the righteousness of Christ, which we get from him, and practice for the glory of His name. Our daily experience lived through the church must be focused on purging out the corruption that grows within us, not for the sake of avoiding punishment, but rather to be purified and united in the body of Christ. It is through this purging that we come to realize that our salvation is made possible through the person of Christ.

A Fifteenth Epistle?

We all know that St. Paul wrote 14 epistles which are recorded in the Bible. However, in verses 9-11, St. Paul reveals that in fact he wrote another epistle to the Corinthians! This epistle also discussed sexual immorality, a problem which seems to have persisted within this particular community. However, this epistle did not survive till today and the content of it is unknown. In Colossians 4:6, there are more reports of lost epistles which were not incorporated in the New Testament.

Sexuality immorality was distorting the community and this caused a division within the community. A division within the community means a division within the body of Christ and the body of Christ can never be divided. This is why St. Paul sought to fix this issue. The unity of the community was the most important thing for St. Paul. This unity can only be achieved through the Eucharistic gathering of the entire community. He would address this in more detail in chapter 11. St. Paul stresses the unity of the body and this is done through the purity of mind and spirit. We are called to live a life in purity in the body of Christ. Christ said, "I am the way, the truth and life". Once we are united in the body of Christ then our life becomes the way, the truth and life to others. Unity is important in order to maintain Christ presence in our lives constantly.

What the Fathers Say

The way the incense give pleasure to the nose, purity would bring gladness to the Holy Spirit, and let Him come to dwell in man.

- St. Ephraim the Syrian

REFLECTION

Whenever a lustful thought enters my mind, do I pray that God removes it straight away? Let us flee from the devil and run to God in prayer.

CHAPTER SIX

CHAPTER SIX

ALL THINGS ARE LAWFUL FOR ME?

Paul continues on the theme of sexual immortality and judging others in chapter six. I want to stress a few verses here that jump out and deal with what we have mentioned in previous chapters. Verse 12 says, "All things are lawful for me, but all things are not helpful. All things are lawful for me, but I will not be brought under the power of any". This verse sums up the entire chapter because Paul is saying everything in creation created by God is good however, we must discern what is harmful for us so that we can transform it into good.

One example is the story I mentioned previously with St. Moses. He was called upon to judge a young monk. Now judging is not bad at all. But rather the way we use judgement can hurt us and others. Judgement is used either to correct someone who is not aware of an action he commits or to convict someone who has done a wrong action. The issue with the story in St. Moses was that the other monks wanted to condemn the monk who was trying to achieve the same thing as the other monks. St. Moses did not think it was fair to cast unfair judgement on this monk. All things are lawful for me but all things are not helpful.

The important point from this verse is to know that God acts through all but we must be careful that our actions and thoughts are not high jacked by being used to hurt others.

This famous verse where St. Paul reminds the people that although something is lawful it does not necessarily mean it is helpful, can be applied to many thing in life. Let's take smoking for example. Is it illegal or unlawful? No. But is it helpful? Certainly not! It is actually extremely unhelpful! Likewise wasting time doing nothing and being lazy... is it a crime? No. But is it helpful? Certainly not! If anything, idle time is a recipe for disaster. Even some of the biggest heroes of the Bible including King David fell when they were lazy.

Verse 17 concludes this chapter beautifully when St. Paul says, "But he who is joined to the Lord is one spirit with Him". Once we are joined to the Lord everything we do reflects our actions in the body of

'Suing the Brethren'

Due to the great division in Corinth, many of the community brought accusations against others in court. St. Paul condemns this and reminds them that God is the just judge. Does this mean that when someone commits a crime against me, I allow it to occur? Certainly not. Everything in the epistle must be read in context. In the time of the Corinthians, extremely small and insignificant matters were the cause of large divisions and therefore St. Paul criticises them.

People, Places &Things

What the Fathers Say

"The Corinthians, who used to boast of their wisdom, and who were assumed to be better than any others; because of the dissensions among them, of which the church suffered, they could not find even one wise man who is able to judge the cases of the brethren without resorting to the pagan courts"

-Origen

Christ. This is why we must be careful when discerning the actions we do. Our actions have the power to unite others in the body of Christ and if our actions are not in the spirit then we become disunited from the body. We must always seek him who died for us on the cross because it was through his death that we have life in his spirit. It is through his resurrection that we live in the joy of the resurrection. Once we seek him through the spirit we find peace and joy in being united to him. Through the spirit we are not only united to him but we are also united to the church. The church being the gathering of the community allows us to be united to our brothers and and sisters in the body of Christ. Through this unity we can discern what is lawful for us and what leads us to Christ.

OUR BODY: TEMPLE OF THE HOLY SPIRIT

St. Paul concludes the chapter by reminding the Corinth community and us

Some More Context

Another interesting contextual fact is that the reading of the letters in the Ancient world would not have been read the same way we read letters today. A great majority of the people were illiterate and could not read the letters of Paul. The letters were read out loud to the community by the priest or deacon of the church being addressed in the letter. It could be done in one sitting it could be done in a couple of sittings.

that 'your body is the temple of the Holy Spirit who is in you'. God purchased us with a price, and therefore we should always remember to imitate him at all times. Our bodies are not for our own pleasure or satisfaction, but instead to glorify God and to live in His image.

The story of St. Perpetua, the first female martyr, is the perfect example of this. Even when she was being tortured by the soldiers in the arena and her clothes were being ripped, she insisted on covering her nakedness with her torn clothes. This was so that she would not be a stumbling block for anyone. We should remember the stories of the saints and how desperate they were to maintain the sanctity of their bodies.

What the Fathers Say

"The salvation of Israel has been through the sea; and the salvation of the whole world is realized through the washing by the word of God"

-St. Cyril of Jerusalem

REFLECTION

How can we learn and remember that our bodies are temples for the Holy Spirit? boys should read the stories of the female saints and likewise, girls should do the same with the male saints.

CHAPTER SEVEN

CHAPTER SEVEN

TWO SHALL BECOME ONE

Chapter seven has St. Paul speaking about marriage. Marriage is a very important practice within the church and in order to understand why St. Paul spends an entire chapter speaking about it we must understand marriage. Marriage is the union of a man and a woman in the body of Christ. The two become one and are united by the spirit. Marriage is a marytria (Greek word meaning sacrifice) to the other individual. We are constantly called to die daily in our marriage. Just like we are called to die to Christ and are given new life, we must also die in our marriage in order to receive new life. This is why the church sees marriage as one of the sacraments because it is a mystery that Christ spoke about.

In those days when the church was still being founded, there were many unbelieving couples where one of the partners later decided to come to the faith. St. Paul encourages the Corinthians to maintain these marriages and not to separate. He explains this by saying: 'For the unbelieving husband is sanctified by the believing wife and the unbelieving wife is sanctified by the believing husband'. However, the believing person must try as hard as possible to bring their unbelieving partner to Christ. This raises the question. Does this mean that marrying an unbeliever is acceptable in our church? Certainly not! For marriage is where man and woman come together and are united by Christ. How can a marriage be sanctified if Christ is not the head of the marriage? St. Paul makes specific exception to those non-Christian couples who are already married where one of them becomes a Christian and not the other.

MISUNDERSTANDING OF MARRIAGE

Sadly, the understanding of marriage in our society today is covered up under labels such as, "she/he is the one", "we are meant to be" and the list can go on. The truth about marriage is forgotten because marriage today is not seen as a restoration to the person of Christ. The life in Christ is life, death and resurrection. Everything we

Celibacy or Marriage?

St. Paul's personal preference is celibacy and consecrating his body for God alone. However, he calls this 'a gift from God' that is not given to all people. Just as celibacy was sanctified by saints such as St. Anthony and St. Demiana, so too was marriage sanctified at the Wedding in Cana of Galilee. Likewise, many saints including St. Peter and St. Rebecca were married and were still able to dedicate their lives to Christ.

People, Places &Things

What the Fathers Say

"Paul proclaims that marriage according to the Word of God is equal to the purity of the holy virginity; saying: "I wish that all men were even as I myself".Those, whom God unites in matrimony, abide in commandment saying: "Husbands, love your wives, just as Christ also loved the Church"

– Origen

do, including marriage, is life, death and resurrection. If we understand marriage from this perspective then true beauty will be found not in the physical senses but from the perspective of Christ who blessed the wedding of Cana. If we continue to look at marriage as a concern to those who "only" are getting married and as something that happens "only" to "them" and we do not see the church involved in the marriage process, therefore, we will never understand the sacramental meaning of marriage and we won't understand the mystery which St. Paul speaks about in Ephesians 5.

By understanding marriage through the unity of man and women within the context of the church, only then will Christ be present blessing the marriage however, if we continue to understanding marriage as concerns for "them" then the kingdom of God will never truly be present in our lives.

REFLECTION
Just as a married couple should try as hard as possible to remain in peace, so too should we try to preserve peace with everyone we encounter.

CHAPTER EIGHT

CHAPTER EIGHT

LOVE TRUMPS KNOWLEDGE

Paul proceeds to talk about knowledge and love. The people of Corinth were fairly knowledgeable people and took pride in this. However, St Paul wishes to teach them and us that love is much more important than knowledge. He states that "Knowledge puffs up but love edifies". Have you ever been in an argument, an you know you are right and the other person is wrong? What is the benefit of being right, if in the end it's just going to cause a problem. In the end (and in almost every argument), both parties lose. Wouldn't it just be better to let it lie and keep the unity?

PAUL ASSERTS HIS AUTHORITY

There was a bit of disagreement in Corinth at the time, regarding eating the meat which is offered to idols. Paul offers a seamlessly simple explanation saying that idols are nothing. There is only one God and he does not live in the idols that you see around you. Paul then starts to assert his authority. He says that even if there were gods in heaven or earth there is only one Father that controls the show. Following this Paul really starts to get smart on the community. He tells them to grow up and forget these silly games. Food does not commend us to God. We do not become better or worse if we eat this kind of food.

But Paul in his complete authority does not just leave it at this. He concludes the chapter by telling the community that not everyone may understand this. Paul says that you must be careful of those who do not have your knowledge. We must even go further out of our way for our brothers and sisters. He says that "if meat makes my brother stumble, I will never again eat meat".

What does he mean? He means that we should take caution that no one looks to us, and because of our actions ends up stumbling. This is the main point from this chapter. If our brother or sister will be scandalized by our actions because they are still young in their faith we must be aware of this and be careful not to scandalize them. We must learn to live for others. And the

What the Fathers Say

"It is the law of Christ Himself, that man should endure the burden of another; By Christ's love you can easily endure his weakness. And even he whom you don't love because of his unbecoming attributes, you should remember that Christ also died for him.

–St. Augustine

Offering to Idols

Whenever an animal was sacrificed in the pagan tradition, one third was burned, one third went to the offerer and one third went to the priest. Priests often sold their portions at temple meat markets. The major issue the Corinthians had was whether or not this meat was contaminated, another cause of much debate and controversy amongst this already divided community.

People, Places &Things

"meat" can be anything! If a kid who looks up to you sees you swearing, they will think it is okay to swear, and then that is on our head!

What the Fathers Say

"Knowledge of a good kind is a servant of love. Knowledge without love puffs up; but love fills the heart, where knowledge finds no void by which it would be puffed up".

–St. Augustine

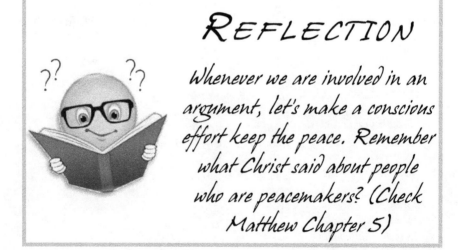

REFLECTION

Whenever we are involved in an argument, let's make a conscious effort keep the peace. Remember what Christ said about people who are peacemakers? (Check Matthew Chapter 5)

CHAPTER NINE

BAPTIZING ALL NATIONS

Chapter nine takes on a different tone compared to the other chapters. St. Paul is asserting his authority in this chapter. He uses the community as his evidence for his work and his apostleship. However, by using his authority and evidence for his apostleship he encourages the community to become servants for all. His hard work is not to comfort people but rather to bring people to Christ. St. Paul is living out the message of Christ by going out and baptizing all nations as Christ commanded in the gospel of Matthew (Chapter 28). This explains why Paul said to the Jews he became a Jew in order that he might win the Jews. This is exactly how we ought to reach all nations today.

PAUL'S SACRIFICE

Paul is trying to show the community that by the mere fact of being a human being Paul had the right and authority to do many things but choice to sacrifice it in the name of the Lord. He has the right to live from the gospel but instead he chose to work for the living so as not to be a burden to those within the ministry. He had the right to take along a believing wife as the other apostles did yet he denied himself this right to dedicate himself completely to ministry. He had the right to be free yet he chose to deny himself this liberty of living a life filled with luxuries and instead became a servant to all that he might win all to Christ. He had the right to walk as a strong man does but instead he chose to become weak to win those who are weak in order to bring more to salvation. All of this was done by Paul to unite the community, a community he is fighting to maintain this unity that has been broken from within.

A more modern example is Anba Abraam. This more modern saint was famously known as the "friend of the poor". He became one of them, in order to win them all to Christ. He only wore a faded garment, which was so shabby that someone felt the need to buy him a new garment (which Anba Abraam promptly gave to a cold beggar he was passing by). He would eat bread and lentils. He would give all he had. One day, a poor woman asked for help, and Anba Abraam did not have money. So he immediately took off his shawl and gave it to her. He made himself a servant to all, just as St Paul did. To the poor, he made himself a poor man– and in doing so he gained riches in heaven!

What the Fathers Say

That is how the blessed Paul became everything for everyone; not to gain some benefit; but, by losing a portion, he may win all.

- St. Cyril the Great

People, Places & Things

Barnabas

St. Paul defends his apostleship and states that he has denied himself of food, drink and a wife for the sake of the service and the zeal for God. He then questions: 'Is it only Barnabas and I who have no right to refrain from working?'. But who exactly is Barnabas? Barnabas was one of Paul's traveling companions and fellow missionaries, joining Paul in spreading the Gospel among the Gentiles. He defends Paul at the council in Jerusalem (Acts 15) and gives an account of Paul's actions because Paul is still not trusted by some of the people.

We too can learn from this. Maybe these days, there aren't as many financially poor people in this country which has financial support to those who need it. But there are definitely many, many people who are lonely and poor when it comes to friends.

What the Fathers Say

In every situation, the Savior, Himself, became everything for everyone, To the hungry he became bread; to the thirsty, water; to the dead, resurrection; to the sick, a Physician; and to the sinners, salvation.

–St. Cyril of Jerusalem

REFLECTION

When was the last time you spoke to or even greeted someone lonely? Let's try imitate Anba Abram and St. Paul and be friends to those who have no friends.

CHAPTER TEN

CHAPTER TEN

TABLE FELLOWSHIP

St. Paul is returning back to the topic of food that he began to address in chapter eight. Paul's concern seems to be set on the table fellowship that became an issue for this particular community. By breaking the meal at the table fellowship, Paul takes issue with this particular practice. He concludes in chapter ten for conscience sake to eat the meat offered at the table. Paul asks the community a simple question at the end of chapter ten. Why I am being judged by another man? Why is evil spoken over the food that has been given thanks? At the end of the day it is God who has the final say and authority. Paul concludes by saying everything you do, do for the glory of God. The breaking up of the table fellowship is an issue Paul is telling them to grow up and come together and eat! He repeats again in this chapter that everything is lawful for us but not everything edifies.

St. Paul is trying to show the community that if all of creation is given to us by God then it has been made holy and if we understand creation as being holy then anything we come into contact with can be made holy. This is the central point in this chapter and we must understand this in the practical sense for our modern times. We have always been taught growing up that certain things are wrong and certain things are bad and this is excellent parenting. However, as we grow older and become critical thinkers it is important to realize that everything has been given to us by God in order that we can not only see the good in it but to share it with others as it was always meant to be from the beginning. God created human beings so that they are not lonely. Everything we do is meant to be shared, done within community in love and brings us together in Christ. St. Paul is trying to stop the disunity that is happening in the community and this chapter ten is a real wake up call for them as it should be for us. It is good to have close friends from the church and to share in the love of Christ but what good does that do for us if we don't share it with those who have no one to love them?

THE EXAMPLE OF ISRAEL

In the first few verses of this chapter, Paul uses the example of the Israelites to warn us. The Israelites, led by Moses, were taken out of Egypt. They experienced

Moses and the Israelites

In Chapter 10, St. Paul uses the story of the Israelites wandering in the wilderness to compare the Jews of the Old Testament with the believers in the New Testament (both the Corinthian community and many of the Christian faithful).

He says that despite all God's miracles (the ten plagues, parting of the Red Sea, manna from heaven and the list goes on), the Israelites continuously rebelled against God and even made for themselves a golden calf to worship (Exodus 32).

People, Places &Things

What the Fathers Say

"In every situation, the Savior, Himself, became everything for everyone, To the hungry he became bread; to the thirsty, water; to the dead, resurrection; to the sick, a Physician; and to the sinners, salvation. "

– Ambrosiaster

the miracle of the Crossing of the Red Sea, passing through water like we did at Baptism. They ate the manna, and we have the Body of Christ. They drank of the Rock, which St Paul tells us was Christ, and we drink the Blood of Christ. And yet, the majority of them were not well pleasing to God. They ended up falling and worshipping the calf, and commited sexual immorality. I always found it very astounding that these people could have such an intimate encounter with God, and have witnessed the Crossing of the Red Sea, and then fall into sin.

But don't we do the exact same thing? Do we not have His Body and Blood every week, and then fall into sins? So St Paul tells us that these are written for out admonition. And he warns us that pride comes before the fall in vs 12 ("Therefore let him who thinks he stands take heed lest he fall"). He tells us to "escape" from temptation. I remember a priest told us, that he had a youth confessing to him,

Solomon

In St. Paul's warning against following after bodily pleasures and desires, he recalls those in the Old Testament who God 'was not pleased with'. Perhaps one of the greatest examples of this is Solomon, the son of King David. Solomon started off his reign very well and pleased God by building the temple. However, gradually he became attracted to earthly pleasures and lusts, and whatever his eyes desired, he received. He ended his life having married 700 women with an additional 300 concubines, and his lust was almost out of control. When nearing his death, Solomon realised that all worldly attractions are 'vanity of vanities and grasping of the wind', a phrase repeated thirty-seven times in the book of Ecclesiastes.

that he fell into a particular sin after a long time of not falling in it. So Abouna asked him what happened? And the youth replied that the day he fell into the sin, he had thought to himself, I have overcome the sin. He had become complacent and had developed a bit of pride, and sure enough he fell.

Notice how St Paul tells us to "escape" from temptation. He doesn't tell us to stand up and reason or argue with Satan. Or to try to debate it... He says "escape". To flee! To run away. But is that cowardly? Am I "chickening out" when I run away from sin? No! Definitely not! What did Joseph in the Old Testament do when Potiphar's wife tried to tempt him? He left his garment and fled! He didn't take any chances. And we count him as a hero of purity.

What the Fathers Say

"As the cloud, being a symbol of the grace of the Spirit has covered the Israelites and protected them against the Egyptians, This same grace is a shield that protects us against the tricks of the devil.

- Ignatius Patriarch of Constantinople

REFLECTION

How many times have we questioned God or complained to Him? Let's remind ourselves of how God protected the Israelites, and learn to trust him more.

CHAPTER ELEVEN

IMITATE ME

Chapter eleven begins the next part of the letter where St. Paul addresses certain aspects in order to unite the community together. He talks about the thanksgiving meal (Eucharist), he talks about head coverings, the resurrection and love. In this chapter he begins by saying, "Imitate me, just as I imitate Christ". This is a powerful line because everything that we do is done based on the person of Christ. Then he begins to tell the community what is to be done.

HEAD COVERINGS

He first talks about head coverings. Head coverings for St. Paul are important because during the time period he wrote the letter, the Roman Society placed a strong emphasis on head coverings for women. This was not because women were lower citizens than men as we have come to understand today but rather this was the clothing attire during the first century Roman period. St. Paul did not want to scandalize the Gentiles who came to the church so he is simply telling women to remember the heading covering within the church. But why do females still wear scarves (head coverings) today? This is because the female's hair is her crown, and how can we wear our crowns in front of the King of Kings Himself? It is for the same reason that bishops remove their crown while reading the gospel and throughout the Holy Liturgy.

THE EUCHARIST

The last part of the chapter St. Paul discusses the thanksgiving meal (the Eucharist). This is an essential part of every Christian's life, and Christ Himself said 'He who eats my body and drinks my blood abides me and I in Him'. St. Paul tells the people to approach it in a worthy manner because you will be held accountable for your actions. This is why the church today teaches us to fast and be prepared for the Eucharist. We fast in preparation that we approach the Eucharist in a worthy manner. Not only is fasting, the physical aspect is needed for preparation but the spiritual aspect is important to be made worthy. This is why developing a routine of going to confession is important in order to maintain a healthy prayer life. Everything the church teaches us is connected and relates to the Eucharist. All the sacraments

What the Fathers Say

"By not covering her head to imitate men a woman would not have the honor of men, as much as losing her own honor"

– St. John Chrysostom

'Each One Takes His Own Supper'

In the first century, many wealthy individuals had poorer 'clients', essentially slaves who helped the wealthy and owed them many different duties. In verse 21, St. Paul writes: 'For in eating, each one takes his own supper ahead of others'. Here, St. Paul describes the corruption of the wealthy, who served their clients and inferior meal after the iimportant people were served.

People, Places &Things

are completed with the partaking of the Eucharist. This is why Christ is the main person we look to because it is in the Eucharist that we become one in his body and we are united to everyone in the body of Christ.

Remember the story of the woman who had a flow of blood for 12 years in Luke 8. She had an ongoing bleeding problem for 12 years, and had become desperate after trying to get help from doctors and failing. So she went and sought to be healed by Jesus. Jesus was surrounded by a multitude of people, so she went and touched the hem of Jesus' garment and was healed. Jesus stopped and asked who had touched Him. His disciple Peter said that there were heaps of people there, obviously someone had touched Him. But Jesus was talking specifically about her.

'The Eucharist'

The word 'Eucharist' (Holy Communion) is the Greek translation for the word 'thanksgiving'. The Eucharist is considered 'the sacrament of sacraments' in the Orthodox Church, and is the central aspect of our faith. The Passover meal was originally a supper to commemorate Israel being from slavery in Egypt. However, Christ transformed the act into a remembrance of him: his life, death and resurrection. Christ is the new Passover Lamb who freed us from slavery of evil and death and leads us into the eternal kingdom of heaven.

Likewise, every Sunday, hundreds of us go up to have Holy Communion. However, how many of us have really touched Him like this woman, and how many of us are just going through the motions like the multitude who were around Him that day?

What the Fathers Say

"Paul reminds us of how the Lord has delivered everything, for our sake; while we refrain from contributing a little food to our fellow believers. When you approach the sacrifice of thanksgiving, give thanks for the sake of what you enjoy, and do not cut yourself off your brethren.

- St. John Chrysostom

REFLECTION

This week, let's prepare ourselves for Communion. Let's get up early, have had confession recently, as we come to have His Body and Blood.

CHAPTER TWELVE

THE GIFTS OF THE SPIRIT

CHAPTER TWELVE

This is powerful chapter because St. Paul is asserting again the reason for writing to the community in Corinth. He is asserting the unity of the spirit. He stresses this by telling them that the spirit unites but everyone who is united to the spirit has different gifts. One is a good speaker; another is a good at serving others etc. There is a diversity of gifts present but they are united in the same spirit. The second point he stresses is unity in the body. He says the body is one however the body has many branches that represent the entire body as one. This is practical because the entire church is united by the Eucharist but everyone has different gifts.

We can find people who are good writers and they contribute to the church magazine. We find people who are good educators so the church gets them to teach Sunday school. The point in all of this is to find your strength and to utilize it for the glory of Christ. If one member is suffering we all suffer. We all need to work hard to ensure the unity of the spirit and this St. Paul does by encouraging those in Corinth to continue to be strong in the spirit.

Spiritual gifts are important for Paul and this is the last section of the epistle to the Corinthians in which he will discuss the spiritual gifts. Paul speaks about spiritual gifts in relation to the church ministry. The apostle presents nine gifts (v. 8-10) all working for the edification of the church. He uses the term body 18 times as a symbol of the church referring to the body of believers living in the body of Christ. The Holy Spirit is the manifestation of these gifts and it is through the working of the spirit that everyone receives the grace to use these gifts. Sadly many were preoccupied with the gift of speaking in tongues as a kind of showing off. We must be careful never to "show off" because this can cause great damage within the community. We must be humble and honest when we approach anyone. His divine salvation is only realized through the work of love.

What the Fathers Say

"No one can have all these gifts, but one will have this, and the other will have that; yet all of them are provided by the same Spirit who gives according to what is convenient for everyone"

- St. Augustine

The Gentiles

Gentiles refer to those people who are not Jewish by birth and therefore are not part of the Jewish community. The Jewish were initially referred to as the people of God, and the Bible says that 'salvation is of the Jews'. However, after Christ's death and resurrection, many of the Gentiles came to the Christian faith, influence by the life of Christ and the teachings of the holy apostles.

People, Places &Things

What the Fathers Say

"Those who got baptized in the early das of the church, for the sake of their salvation used to gain apparent signs of having the grace of the Holy Spirit. Although the Corinthians experienced all that, yet they did not use those gifts for the edification of the church, but only cared for showing them off"

- Theodore of Cyprus

NOT TO LOSE HEART

Some of us may lose heart when we hear the stories of the saints and miracle-performers in the world. However, we should never let these evil thoughts take control over us. St. Paul asks: 'Are all apostles? Are all prophets? Are all teachers? Are all workers of miracles?'. He says this to show that everyone is equal within the church community, emphasising that no one is greater than the other. Even though we may not be prophets or wonder-workers, the sheer fact that God has allowed us to be His children is the greatest blessing imaginable! An act of love is far greater than any miracle or prophecy, and all of us are capable of performing such acts.

REFLECTION

We often use our gifts to serve ourselves only. Today, let's use whatever gift God has given us for the service of others.

CHAPTER THIRTEEN

CHAPTER THIRTEEN

THE MYSTERY OF LOVE

Chapter thirteen connects with chapter twelve. This is because chapter twelve speaks about spiritual gifts while chapter thirteen speaks about the greatest of all spiritual gifts which is love. This chapter is misunderstood today, but has deep understandings that we need to comprehend and apply today. St. Paul begins by saying no matter what we do and how much is done if we do not have love our actions are futile. He then begins to describe what love is. He gives action verbs like "love suffers", "is kind" and "is not puffed up". Mother Teresa said that kindness is not 'large acts of mercy but rather small acts of mercy done with lots of love'. Love could be as simple as visiting a sick friend or speaking to someone who is lonely.

SOCIETY'S VIEW OF LOVE

In our modern society we see many different media outlets that try to tell us what love is and this is good. However what our society can't answer is why divorce rates are over 50 percent and people who supposedly love each other don't anymore after a few years. The simple answer boils down to the understanding of love. If love does not become a sacrifice or martyrdom that is lived out constantly then the relationship won't last or a friendship won't last. If Christ is not present then how can one even begin to think of making the relationship holy and pure? We must realize that love is lived out for the other. Once we realize this and begin to apply it then true love, the kind St. Paul speaks about in this chapter, will be realized by everyone in their lives. This is when Christ will be present and by allowing love to be a sacrifice, you will go more and more each day to love that person more and more. As St. Paul concludes the chapter, "Love never fails". And if love never fails Christ never fails and if Christ does not fail then us humans can never fail either.

What the Fathers Say

"Mentioning the worst and most terrifying kind of death, namely burning, he still says that without love, it would profit him nothing"

- St. John Chrysostom

People, Places &Things

Love:

This whole chapter, as with the epistle in general, is focused on love. The early Christians chose the Geek word 'agape' for love and filled it with new meaning. There are four main types of love.

1. Family love ('Storghay')

This is the type of love which is a result of living with someone for many years or knowing that you are closely related to them.

LOVE AS A COMMITMENT

What the Fathers Say

"Even if you perform miracles, if you keep your virginity, if you keep on fasting and praying, yet you are suffering from the pains of envy, you will certainly be worse than all sinners"

- St. John Chrysostom

In this chapter the spirit reveals the commitment of the believer to love, in order to benefit from the spiritual gifts; as without love, the gifts would not be useful and they would make one lose hope in this life. This chapter does an excellent job to prepare us for the speaking of tongues which has been abused within the Corinthian community. Love is opening the heart to bear Christ and through it, man can love all mankind beyond limits and restrictions. Love is not to admire another, nor to get along well with another. It is giving with all possibilities for the sake of everyone, without expecting anything in return, but to love for the sake of God who himself is love. As long as God is love and God and Christ are one then our understanding of love is made known through Christ. We can even substitute the word love for Christ

2. Friendship Love ('Phileo'):

This is the type of love which develops if you share something in common with someone. For example, you and your friend might like soccer and talk about it and watch games together.

3. Romantic Love ('Eros'):

This is the type of love which comes from emotional and physical attraction and is best developed between a husband and wife.

4. Charitable Love: ('Agape'):

This is the greatest type of love where you intentionally decide to share it freely with everyone.

and our understanding will be made clear.
Christ's love was manifested for all through
his birth, death and resurrection.

REFLECTION

We can't all do large acts of mercy, but today, let's do small acts of mercy with lots of love for our brothers and sisters.

CHAPTER FOURTEEN

AUTHORITY OF CHRIST

CHAPTER FOURTEEN

In this chapter St. Paul is asserting that when teaching is done that a high authority needs to be present in order to interpret what is being taught. There seems to have been a lot of divisions created in this community not just at the thanksgiving meal but also in teachings that were taught by certain individuals. We must learn to listen and to take our information from those who the church deems as being educated in the faith and understand all the doctrines.

Some of us today listen to a lot of Christian pastors and are influenced heavily by the rise of mainstream evangelical Christian movements. The issue is not so much in listening to them but rather we are still young in our faith and understanding to discern what is correct teaching or what is not. Unfortunately many today profess that they are teaching correct teachings when they are not. We must approach religious education or theology with much care and guidance from priests or bishops who have been trained in the faith. This is why having a spiritual father is of the utmost importance so they can guide us.

PURSUIT OF LOVE

St Paul then focuses on the abuse that has occurred in misusing the spiritual gifts. Speaking in tongues is an issue St. Paul looks to correct and adopts a strict method to who can teach and speak within the community. He begins by telling them to pursue love. Love, as we have established, is the most important gift that controls all other gifts. If we do not have pure love then the spiritual gifts will be abused.

Many always wonder why a priest or a spiritual father is hard on the community. This is not to make people feel ashamed or to drive the out of the church but rather it's used as a teaching tool. Just like a parent is hard on their kids to teach them, likewise a priest can be too, and St Paul does the same here. St. Paul makes it clear that the only way

<u>Women</u>

In verse 34, St. Paul demands: 'Let your women keep silent in the churches, for they are not permitted to speak. Did St. Paul have anything against women? Certainly not!

Once again the context of this statement is *important. Certain women within the city of Corinth were being disruptive during their worship and causing many problems, and therefore St. Paul orders them to keep silent. However, St. Paul actually encouraged women to pray and prophesy in church in chapter 11.*

People, Places &Things

What the Fathers Say

"The apostle compares between the greater and the lesser gift (speaking with tongues); showing that the later are neither completely useless, nor greatly beneficial. But the Corinthians were actually puffed up because they thought speaking in tongues was a great gift"

-St. John Chrysostom

to use the spiritual gifts correctly is by pursing love. We must learn to pursue love in order to live in the body of Christ. Christ's death and resurrection was the culmination of love and in dying and rising we are made by God out of love. We have become the definition of love by being made in His image and likeness. We must learn to pursue love in order that others might see Christ working within us.

A famous example of a spiritual father being harsh is the story of Anba Bemwa, who showed little mercy on his disciple St.John the Short. Anba Bemwa ordered St. John the Short to go to the wilderness, catch a wild hyena and bring it to him. This was done as a test of his obedience. A few hours later, he returned with the hyena to Anba Bemwa. Anba Bemwa marvelled at the obedience of his disciple. Anba Bemwa, out of love for his disciple, did not want him to fall in the sin of pride. He reprimanded him saying: 'This is

Tongues

In the Roman world, epileptics were considered to have the 'divine disease'. The people thought that epileptics were possessed by a god, and their meaningless speech was actually the god's message!

The similarities between those who spoke in tongues and epileptics led the Corinthians to believe that those who spoke in tongues had a divine spiritual gift. However, St. Paul placed more emphasis on the preacher's words being understood so that the believers and

non-believers could act accordingly.

a dog, and not a hyena'. St. John the Short humbly accepted his father's criticism even though it clearly was not true. Close to his death, Anba Bemwa said: 'St. John the Short has become an angel amongst men'.

REFLECTION

Many problems within the Corinth community arose as a result of people 'speaking in tongues'. For today, let's learn to listen more and to teach less.

CHAPTER FIFTEEN

THE HOPE OF RESURECTION

CHAPTER FIFTEEN

Chapter fifteen is the second last chapter and essentially St. Paul tries to tie up all his previous points in this chapter. This is the culmination of everything he spoke to the community beforehand. He challenges the people in the community because it seems that they had taken a lax understanding to the resurrection of Christ and it explains why St. Paul is speaking in an apologetic manner in this chapter. He tells them that if the resurrection had not happened then everything I have told you are not true and if Christ not did not rise from the dead then there is no hope in this life or the next. The resurrection is important and in order to live out the message of Christ we must understand the resurrection. Within the church the most important feast day is the feast of Resurrection (Easter). Not only does this day commemorate Christ's resurrection but it also remembers Christ defeating death and restoring humanity in the image and likeness of God.

The resurrection then is a joyful event. The church is covered in white and all the hymns are chanted in the joyful tune. It is the one feast in the church we celebrate for fifty days and the church is in a joyous time period during the Holy Fifty. This means that the resurrection is the joy that makes Christians unite in the body of Christ. If Christianity is the religion of joy then we must learn to be joyful and in us being joyful we naturally live out the resurrection of Christ every day. I remember once a bishop said, "If we are the people of the good news then why are we so grim?" We must learn to be joyful in all actions because everything we act on leads us to Christ. His resurrection allows us to live a holy life. We must purify our minds in order to see Christ all in all.

EVIL COMPANY CORRUPTS GOOD HABITS

St Paul reminds us of a startling fact in vs 33: evil company corrupts good habits. In other words, if you hang around with the wrong crowd, you will develop bad habits. We all know this. If you hang around friends who swear a lot, you may end up swearing. We are all easily influenced by those around us. Why take that risk then? If my friends are going to a club or any other place where I might be drawn to sin, why go? Why tiptoe so near to a potential sin? If

'Death Destroyed'

St. Paul questions 'O death where is your sting? O Hades, where is your victory?', even exclaiming that 'death is swallowed up in victory'. This points to the prophesy made by Isaiah in the Old Testament (25: 8), 'He will swallow up death forever, And the Lord God will wipe away tears from all faces'. After much stern warning and judgement, St. Paul reminds the Corinthians and us of the ultimate goal in our life. This shows the unity of the Old Testament and the New Testament.

People, Places &Things

What the Fathers Say

"The evils of the sinners are not greater than the righteousness of Him who died for their sake. The sins committed were not greater than the justice that was realized when He delivered His life for our sake"

- St. Cyril of Jerusalem

you see a big, muddy, ditch in the ground, do you tiptoe around the edge, or do you steer clear? We steer clear.

So why take the risk when it comes to my spiritual life? By the same token, if we hang around friends who are close to the church, we also will be close to the church. I remember Fr Dawood Lamey speaking to a group of youth, and telling them to "Hang around friends who open the Bible easily". When we do that, then we too will open the Bible easily.

In Psalm 1, David the prophet writes: 'Blessed is the man who walks not in the counsel of the ungodly, nor stands in the path of sinners, nor sits in the seat of the scornful'. Notice the progression of the verbs: 'walks', 'stands' and 'sits'. When someone 'sits' with the sinners, they consciously make a decision to surround themselves by evil company. However, our goal as Christians is to 'walk' past the sinners

The Resurrection

Many of the Corinthians struggled to grasp this concept of resurrection. The main reason why is because this thought was not popular in Greek philosophical thought. In Greek philosophy, the emphasis was placed on the spiritual over the physical- making the resurrection something that did not make a lot of sense to the community members and avoid surrounding ourselves with any sort of evil. The psalm goes on to describe this person as prosperous and successful in everything he does. Meanwhile, the ungodly 'shall not stand in judgement'.

In today's society, 'evil company' is not limited to being around a bad group of friends alone.

'Evil company' could come in the form of an inappropriate TV show or movie. For just as being around a bad group of friends places within our minds bad thoughts and ideas, so too do inappropriate TV shows and films pollute our minds with sin. Whenever an evil thought enters into our mind as a result of such exposure, then the devil may eventually develop this thought into a sinful action. Therefore, it is recommended to avoid all kinds of 'evil company'.

REFLECTION

Today, let's try and avoid all kinds of evil company, whether this is a bad group of friends or an inappropriate TV show.

CHAPTER SIXTEEN

CHAPTER SIXTEEN

SEEK CHRIST IN ALL

The final concluding chapter deals with tithing. St. Paul wants the saints to give generously for those who are struggling. We must learn to share with others so that we can all share in the glory of Christ. Giving money is not the only method of tithing but also giving your time and talents to serve others falls under the category of tithing. God in Malachi chapter 3 says that by not paying their tithes, they had insulted God. And He promises overflowing rewards for paying tithes.

One of the desert fathers had only a single possession, a Bible from which he contemplated on by day and night. His brother came to him and asked him for the Bible. Upon giving it to him, the father said 'I gave away the same book which told me to sell all I have and give to the poor' and was satisfied, even though he had lost the only thing he had.

Paul concludes the chapter with a farewell and he will see the community soon. Having dealt with the dogmatic and social problems in the church, openly and firmly, St. Paul concludes the epistle wisely, by proclaiming his love for them. He begins with words of love and encouragement, and ended it with holy greetings so that he concluded the epistle the same way he began it. He also proclaims his wish to visit them (v.5-9), sends Timothy and tells them about Apollo's visit to them. He ends by telling them to greet one another with a holy kiss, and to receive his love for them in Christ. The holy kiss is very important because it shows the love that we have for each other. This practice is still used to this day when during the liturgy we offer each other the kiss of peace through the touching of the hands. This should be a joyous occasion as we "literally" greet each other in love.

Even though Paul is not present, this is what he intends for the community when he wrote that. These all are works of love exchanged between those who labor in the vineyard and the congregation they minister; and in between each of these categories among themselves; the church of Christ would grow in them!

What the Fathers Say

"Paul exhorts them to be brave and strong as wrestlers and soldiers of Christ, yet to do everything with love for God and one another"

-St. Dedymus the blind

Method of Writing

St. Paul concludes the epistle with greetings and reaffirms his desire to visit the Corinthians soon. However, the way St. Paul writes Corinthians, as with most of his other epistles, is extremely interesting. St.

Paul would dictate to a scribe, who would then write down on a piece of paper. At the end, if necessary, he would add a note with his own hand. The New Testament writers followed this habit, as shown in Romans 16:22 (see also 2 Thessalonians 3:17).

People, Places &Things

What the Fathers Say

"Knowing for sure that all the treasures of the riches of heaven are found in Christ, he writes "The grace of our Lord Jesus be with You. Here he prays for the grave of Christ alone, without adding the word 'God', for he is convinced that the grace of God is itself the grace of Christ"
-St. Dedymus the blind

St. Paul then concludes the epistle with the seemingly frightening verse: 'If anyone does not love the Lord Jesus Christ, let him be accursed'. He had laboured daily with tears to create harmony and unity between the Corinthians. However, at the end of the day, salvation is a choice and a forward step which I have to make. It is true that Christ stands knocking at the door, but we must be the ones who open the door and allow him to enter. In the icon of Christ knocking on the door, the door knob is depicted on the inside of the door only, meaning that I am the one who is meant to allow Christ's entry.

REFLECTION

How many times has Christ knocked on the door when I've been too busy. Today, let's spend a bit more time praying or reading our Bibles?

CPSIA information can be obtained
at www.ICGtesting.com
Printed in the USA
LVHW031942011218
598945LV00001B/76